THE ART OF MINING

Gosforth Colliery, 'On the west bank of a romantic dean, through which the Ouse Burn winds its way to the Tyne'.

The sinking of Gosforth colliery began in 1825 and the first coal was won in 1829, an event celebrated by a 'grand subterranean ball'. On the 6th of February 1829 almost 300 people descended into the pit:

The ball-room, which was situated at the depth of nearly 1,100 feet below the surface of the earth, was in the shape of an L … the floor was flagged, and the whole place was brilliantly illuminated with lamps and candles. The company began to assemble and descend … in the morning … Immediately on their arrival at the bottom of the shaft, they proceeded to the face … where each person hewed a piece of coal … As soon as a sufficient number of guests had descended, dancing commenced, and continued without intermission till three o'clock in the afternoon, when all ascended once more … The Coxlodge band was in attendance; and cold punch, malt liquor, and biscuits of all kinds were in abundance.

From *Sykes' Local Records*, quoted by Thomas Hair.

THE ART OF MINING

Thomas Hair's Watercolours of the Great Northern Coalfield

'... we can say in truth that no-where have we met with more *real* politeness than on "the pit-heap".'

Thomas Hair

Douglas Glendinning

TYNE BRIDGE PUBLISHING

in association with the Friends of the Hatton Gallery, University of Newcastle upon Tyne

Acknowledgements:

Tyne Bridge Publishing at Newcastle Libraries & Information Service would like to thank the Friends of the Hatton Gallery for their invaluable support.

The author would like to thank, for their help and support, above all Kate, Lizzie and Lucy Glendinning; Anna Flowers, Tyne Bridge Publishing; Hatton Gallery; Friends of the Hatton Gallery; Angela and Sue, Fine Art Library, University of Newcastle; Prof. John Milner, University of Newcastle; Beamish Museum; Laing Art Gallery, Newcastle; Local Studies, Newcastle Libraries & Information Service; Newcastle Society of Antiquaries; Stanley Library; Les Golding, Tyne & Wear Museums; Ian Ayris; Tom Callaghan; Anthony and Tim Flowers; Thomas Hair of Liverpool; Vanessa Histon; Paul Mearns; Dr Anthony Parton, University of Durham; Maureen Stephenson; Jean Taylor; Yvonne Vint.

Douglas Glendinning is an art historian, currently lecturing at the University of Durham and with Fairfax University, USA.

Published by
City of Newcastle upon Tyne
Education & Libraries Directorate
Newcastle Libraries & Information Service
Tyne Bridge Publishing, 2000

ISBN: 1 85795 180 8

Printed by Elanders Hindson, North Tyneside

The Hatton Gallery
Admission free
University of Newcastle upon Tyne NE1 7RU
tel/fax: 0191 2226059
www.ncl.ac.uk/hatton

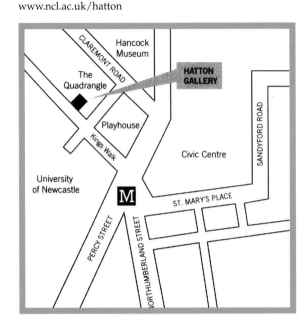

Tyne Bridge Publishing, part of Newcastle Libraries & Information Service, publish a wide range of local history titles featuring the North-East of England. See the complete list at:

www.newcastle.gov.uk/tynebridgepublishing
or request our free catalogue on 0191 2774174

Cover illustrations:

Front cover: Percy Pit, Percy Main Colliery.
Opened in 1807, this pit was one of the most productive on the Tyne. In 1843 the 611 men and boys working there raised 104,550 tons of coal.

Back cover: Water wheel, Beamish Colliery.
The water wheel was used for draining the lower seams of the colliery, which had been opened in 1763. By the 1840s the pit was only partly worked.

Title page: Air shaft, Wallsend Colliery.

Contents

Foreword

In the permanent collection of the Hatton Gallery, University of Newcastle upon Tyne, there exists a remarkable series of watercolour sketches. The paintings provide a unique visual document of social and industrial history of the North-East of England in the early nineteenth century. The images were created by the artist, Thomas Harrison Hair (1810-1875).

Whilst Hair's engravings, as reproduced in his *Sketches of the Coal Mines in Northumberland and Durham*, 1839, and Views *of the Collieries … of Northumberland and Durham*, 1844, have been widely published, the original watercolours from which they were taken have not been on general public display, and rarely reproduced in any publication. As a result, these images are little known.

The primary intention of this book is to introduce Thomas Hair's watercolours to a wider audience. Viewed together, the paintings tell a remarkable story, illustrating the way coal was transported from deep underground to the collier ships which carried these 'black diamonds' to the markets in London and abroad.

Each image in this selection has been chosen to give an insight into the conditions, practices and attitudes prevalent in the coal mining culture in the North-East of England at that time. In the accompanying descriptions, the emphasis has been placed on the use of nineteenth century observations and commentary rather than the interpretations of modern writers.

A short glossary of mining terms

A Newcastle Coal Pit
in the olden time.

Bank: The area around the top of the pit shaft.

Banksman: A man employed at the top of the shaft to hook up and unhook corves and other equipment from the lifting gear servicing the pit shaft.

Brakesman: A man who travelled on wagons rolling down inclines controlling the speed of descent by means of a brake lever fixed to the wagon (see page 42).

Casters: Men employed on the river Wear to transfer coal from the keels to the colliers.

Chaldron: Wagon for carrying coal from the collieries to the staiths along wagonways and railway lines.

A measure of coal: A 'Newcastle chaldron' = approx. 2.5 tons of coal. A 'London chaldron' = approx. 1.5 tons of coal.

Choke damp: Carbon Dioxide.

Coastwise: Coal carried by sea to the various home markets, of which London was the most important.

Colliers: The ships engaged to carry coal to other ports.

Corves: Wicker baskets used to convey the coal from the underground workings to the surface of the colliery. A corve would contain about 560 lbs of coal when full.

Dragsman: A man employed to drag sledges of coal from the pit face.

Drops: Mechanism for loading coal directly into the collier ships and keel boats waiting at the staiths on the river.

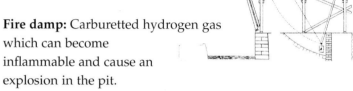

Fire damp: Carburetted hydrogen gas which can become inflammable and cause an explosion in the pit.

Head gear: The arrangement of equipment immediately above the pit shaft to transfer pitmen and equipment to and from the workings and to lift corves or tubs of coal from the mine.

Hewers: Pitmen employed to dig coal at the coalface.

Keelmen: Men who crewed the keel boats or keels, on the rivers.

Keels: Flat-bottomed shallow-draughted boats used to transfer coal from staiths up river to the larger, sea going colliers waiting in deeper water.

Landsale: Coal sold locally for domestic and industrial use. Coal transported over land.

Putters: Young boys, and in some places girls, who conveyed corves of coal through the mine workings on sledges.

Rolley: A low-slung wheeled trolley.

Rolleyway: Rails which carried the rollies.

Safety lamp: A device for providing light in mines without the risk of explosion of a naked flame. After about 1816 the Davy Lamp was widely accepted. The lamp illustrated left was in common use in the 1840s.

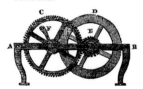

Screens: Mechanism 'at bank' to grade the size of coal and to allow any stone or shale to be removed from the coal.

Sledges: Wooden sledges, sometimes wheeled, on which corves full of coal were transported through the workings.

Staiths: Sites on the river bank where jetties and drops were constructed to load coal from the wagons into the keels and colliers.

Steel mill: Device to create a dim light in the mine workings. A shower of sparks was created by bringing a flint against a revolving steel wheel.

Stink damp: Hydrogen sulphide gas.

Trappers: Some of the youngest mine workers, employed to open and close trap doors in the workings to help control the air flow underground.

Viewer: The colliery manager.

Wagonway: Trackways or railways along which wagons of coal were conveyed from the pits to the staiths. The earliest of the tracks were wooden and the wagons hauled by horses. 'Clap your hands for daddy's coming down the wagonway…' (traditional rhyme).

Whin gin: Horse powered winding device located at the top of the pit shaft to transfer men, equipment and coal through the shaft. May be a corruption of 'winding engine', a mechanism to wind.

*The whin gin above is taken from the frontispiece of Thomas Hair's **Sketches of the Coal Mines …**, 1839.*

*Other illustrations on these two pages are reproduced from Matthias Dunn: **Winning and Working of Collieries**, 1848 and John Holland: **Fossil Fuel, the Collieries and Coal Trade of Great Britain**, 1841.*

Thomas Harrison Hair

Thomas H. Hair was a painter and engraver specialising in landscapes and maritime scenes. However, very little is known about his life. He was born in Newcastle upon Tyne, around 1810, the son of John Hair, a lamp black manufacturer and tanner from Scotswood. His training in art probably began in the workshops of the Tyneside engraver and lithographer, Mark Lambert (1781-1855). Lambert himself had been assistant to the master wood engraver from Cherryburn, Northumberland, Thomas Bewick, 1753-1828.

Genealogists have discovered a tantalising possible link between Thomas Hair and another Northumbrian artist, Luke Clennell (1781-1840). Clennell, a painter and wood engraver, had been apprentice and assistant to Thomas Bewick in Newcastle. His grandmother was Elizabeth Hair of East Sleekburn in Northumberland, the same small village from which Thomas Hair's own grandfather originated.

In the late 1830s Hair went to work in London, where he is known to have lived at two addresses in the Camden Town area. His connections with and interest in his native North-East continued to be strong and were reflected in the subjects of the work he produced during that time, for example: *On the Derwent, Winlaton Mill*, 1842; *The Barque 'Bomarsund' off Tynemouth*, 1857; *The Tyne at Ryton*, 1863; *The Tyne at Scotswood, Northumberland*,1863; *The great International Sculling Match, Newcastle*, 1868.

As well as exhibiting in Newcastle upon Tyne, Hair also showed in London. His paintings were exhibited at the Suffolk Street Gallery from 1838, and at the Royal Academy during the 1840s. Royal Academy submissions included in 1841, *On Tynedale Fell, Cumberland*, in 1844 the wonderfully entitled *Burning for Blood, Long and Gaunt and Grim Assembling of Wolves etc ...*, and in 1849, *Bothwell Castle*.

The works considered in this book form part of a series of watercolour sketches Hair produced between about 1828 and 1842, which includes several years when he was living in London. They are held in the permanent collection of the Hatton Gallery, University of Newcastle upon Tyne. These images were preparatory sketches for etchings that Hair used to illustrate his book, *Views of the Collieries ... of Northumberland*

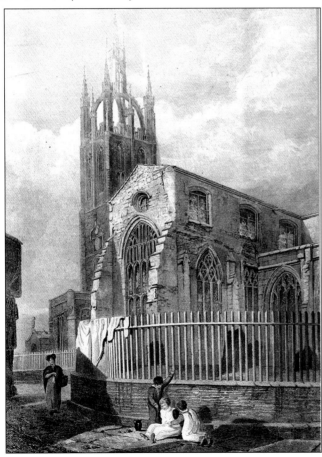

An engraving, c.1840, by Mark Lambert, of St Nicholas's Cathedral.

and Durham, published in 1844. This was a much enlarged edition of his earlier *Sketches of the Coal Mines ...* published in 1839, and included a lengthy, 'Preliminary Essay on Coal and the Coal Trade' by M. Ross, which provides a detailed and illuminating account of the coal industry in the North-East in the first half of the nineteenth century.

Descriptions of each of the forty-two etched illustrations or 'Views' are also included. It must be stressed that the watercolours in the Hatton Gallery were preparatory sketches, and not finished pieces, but this does not in any way diminish the importance of the images. The sketches were intended to provide an accurate record of the essential elements of the scene in front of the artist. Hair needed to record as much information as possible in the watercolours to aid his memory when he made the etchings later, in the studio. As well as being pleasing to look at, the very immediacy of the watercolours means that they convey more of the atmosphere of the working life of the coal mines than the formalised etchings.

Hair's interest in recording collieries began early in his career. The earliest known work by Thomas Hair is *Hebburn Colliery A Pit*, dated 1828, which is in the Hatton collection. Although Hair was only about eighteen years old at the time, his technique as a watercolourist and his eye for detail was well developed for such a young man.

Watercolour is a transparent and quick drying medium. Because mistakes cannot be easily rectified, the artist needs a high degree of skill. The great advantage of working in water-

Hebburn Colliery A Pit, painted in 1828 when Thomas Hair was only 18 years old.

colours was that they were portable. As he toured the coalfield on his open air painting forays, Hair could easily carry a small box of watercolour paints and some brushes. For the most part, the structural elements in the sketches, the timbers of the headgear for example, have been clearly delineated in ink and pencil under drawing, then colour has been applied, generally with some degree of subtlety.

There has possibly been some deterioration in the quality of the pigments in several of the watercolours in the series. In addition, Hair would have used a limited palette of colours because the paintings were to be etched and therefore the tonal range, rather than colour, was most important.

Several of the images have anomalies in their use of perspective. These visual irregularities were usually rectified in

Newcastle, early 1840s, from Gateshead, showing the Brandling Junction Railway. The coal wagons are being drawn up an inclined plane from Redheugh.

the finished etchings but some were left, and this adds a certain quirkiness to their charm.

Little of the work Hair produced after the publication of *Views* deals with the subject of industry so directly. There is the well known *Hartley Colliery, After the Disaster*, c.1869, a view recalling the terrible calamity of January 16 1862, in which 204 men and boys from that small Northumberland village lost their lives. However, the greater part of Hair's artistic output can be categorised as general landscape views. His topographical studies, executed around Newcastle and along the banks of the river Tyne, provide fascinating evidence of the life of the town and the bustle and commerce which transformed the former Roman river crossing point into one of the major economic centres of Victorian Britain.

Although Thomas Hair produced many etchings, engravings and paintings during his long career, the story of the man behind the art remains something of a mystery. The artist's death is registered in Newcastle as 11 August 1875, and not 1882 as frequently stated in biographies. He was buried in an unmarked grave on 13 August in All Saints Cemetery. Paintings attributed to Thomas Hair that are catalogued as having been produced after 1875 will need to be reconsidered.

Art and the Industrial Revolution

The Industrial Revolution was at its height when Thomas Hair created his watercolour sketches, but most artists made no real attempt to record the changes it brought. In many parts of Britain both landscape and society had been radically restructured as a result of industrialisation. Many agricultural workers moved to the developing urban and industrial centres to provide labour for the new industries. Artists, however, rarely depicted the symbols of industrialisation – mills, engineering workshops and railways – and the actual relentless physical toil required by much industrial production. Nor did they examine the social implications of these changes. By and large, art was still concerned with representing the English rural tradition, helping to maintain a sense of continuity within society, no matter how insincere or contrived those representations were. The upper and expanding middle classes who bought art did not want pictures showing the reality of manual labour. Images of young children and women, often malnourished and poorly clothed, shackled to long days of unremitting hard work would not have hung easily on the drawing room walls of the comfortably off.

In the later eighteenth century, Joseph Wright of Derby (1734-1797) did produce a number of images indicating that artists may have begun searching for new subjects that represented the new age, one example is his *Arkwright's Cotton Mill by Night*, painted around 1783. But in truth, regardless of its many attributes, Wright's scene is more romantic by moonlight than dark and satanic. It was left to foreigners visiting Britain in the early nineteenth century such as the German, Carl Schinkel (1781-1841), and the Frenchman, Jean Louis Gericault (1791-1824), to make some effort to record the consequences of industrialisation on British Society.

Painters living and working within the boundaries of the

Dragsmen pull and push a waggon of coal.
*(From Matthias Dunn's **Winning and Working of Collieries, 1848.**)*

North-East coalfield were no more eager than their southern contemporaries to represent the working conditions, poverty and the squalid housing that were prevalent in the region at that time in both agricultural and mining villages – it simply would not have been of interest, and certainly would not have been saleable. Thomas Hair's work does not, in this sense, offer any real impression of the life mining folk endured either at work or at home. Of course it was not possible to 'paint' underground scenes. The view at the bottom of the shaft or where the rollies were loaded – which Hair did paint – was as far as an artist could penetrate into a mine. The seams were low, dark, dangerous and often wet.

Images of coalmining could be found in technical manuals published at the time (as in Matthias Dunn's, above), but they were intended to be illustrative of the ways and means of industrial practice rather than to raise questions about working conditions, or the morality of child labour.

Although 'men' and 'boys' are frequently referred to in this text it is salutary to remember that women and girls had also been employed in the pits of Northumberland and Durham. In the collieries of the North-East, 'the practice had ceased since 1780'. In other coal mining areas the use of female labour underground continued for some years. In 1839 a Royal Commission was established to enquire into the employment of children in coal mines and 'the effects of such employment, both with regard to their morals and their bodily health'. One of the Commissioners reported:

When the nature of the horrible labour is taken into considera-
tion, its extreme severity, its regular duration of between twelve
and fourteen hours daily … and the tender age and sex of the
workers, a picture is presented of deadly physical oppression and
systematic slavery.

Not all of those involved in the management and financial profit of the coal industry shared the Commissioners' opinions. Colliery viewer John Buddle believed that mining should not 'dispense with the service of young boys'. (Child labour was, of course, cheap.) He wrote:

What we have to guard against is any obnoxious legislative
interference in the established customs of our peculiar breed of
Pitmen. The stock can only be kept up by breeding … But if our
meddling, morbid, humanity mongers get it infused into their
heads, that it is cruel unnatural slavery to work in the dark …
twelve hours a day in the pit, a screw in the system would be
loose.

It was believed that the best pitmen were bred to the job and the pitman's skills were handed down through the generations. It was not uncommon for inexperienced child workers' legs to be tied together to prevent them from wandering off and getting lost in the darkness.

An Act of Parliament was passed in 1842 prohibiting the employment of boys younger that ten, and any female, underground in a coal mine. The law was, of course, often disregarded. One chronicler of life and work on the North-East coalfield, J.R. Liefchild, writing in 1850 of his descent into Pemberton Main Colliery, Sunderland, reported talking to a trapper 'who was certainly not above seven years old'. Another 'who seemed to be five or six and all for the daily rate of 10d' (about 4p). Liefchild declared: 'Yes happy mother in your suburban villa and nursery, 10d a day was the price of that child's imprisonment'.

Hair found the pitmen consistently helpful, despite the terrible rigours and impoverishment of the lives of the mining communities. He noted that during the research for his book:

The utmost extent of their [the pit folk] knowledge has always
been freely given; and that we can say in truth that nowhere have
*we been met with more **real** politeness than on the 'pit-heap' .*

Except for the odd glimpse of a figure here and there above ground, lifting a shovel or pushing a tub, Hair's watercolours are also devoid of any notion of the physical hardship and dangers associated with coal mining. Perhaps criticism of Hair. and indeed his fellow artists, for avoiding the starker aspects

A woman and two children haul a tub of coals. Women were not generally
employed in North-East pits after the late eighteenth century.
*(From Matthias Dunn's **Winning and Working of Collieries**, 1848.)*

of life in the Industrial Revolution is unjust. Hair was a professional artist, in that he derived his living from selling the work he produced. The paintings and etchings he created, like the coal he depicted in his sketches, were subject to market forces. The ugly didn't sell. Possibly mindful of what public tastes would tolerate, the opening sentence of the preface to *Sketches* contains an apology from the publisher for the 'uncompromising nature of the subject which he has chosen to illustrate'.

What then was Hair's motivation for producing *Sketches of the Coal Mines*? He says he intends to:

Afford faithful delineations of the various objects associated with the working and shipment of coal, and not, by the introduction of meretricious effects, to produce a display of pictorial beauty at the expense of truth to nature.

In the preface to *Sketches*, it is stated that Hair wished to fill an 'unacceptable vacuum [in] pictorial illustrations' of an industry 'of such importance … in both a local and national point of view' and that occupied a 'prominent position in the scale of national production and commerce'.

The book was not intended for a general readership. The cost of producing an illustrated work like this would make it relatively expensive to buy and the subject would be somewhat specialised. A note in the preface thanks 'a very numerous and highly respectable body of subscribers, amongst whom may be found gentlemen [of] standing in the coal trade both in the metropolis and the north'. These people may be assumed to be the artist's intended audience.

Some acknowledgement of the human cost of winning of coal is made in the text of Hair's book. Typical are the entries concerning Jarrow Colliery:

September 25, 1817, when six men lost their lives.

April 28, 1820, two persons killed.

January 17, 1826 … forty two men and boys were killed, and some others much burnt.

March 15, 1828, eight men lost their lives.

August 3, 1830 … forty two men and boys were deprived of life … leaving widows and sixty six children. Ten more much injured…'.

As any scenes of industry at this time are comparatively uncommon, the information that can be gleaned from accurate representations are all the more valuable. Hair's detailed observations of the coal industry of the early 1800s are without equal and are highly reliable sources of reference to historians and industrial archaeologists.

From **The Miners' Advocate** *edited by William Daniells, 1843-1845. Previously the* **Miners' Journal**, **The Miners' Advocate** *was written for the 'ill-paid, ill-used, and oppressed Colliers and Miners of Great Britain and Ireland'. The illustration shows 'the collier in one of the most laborious of his occupations—viz.: removing his tools'.*

The original edition of Thomas Hair's book was illustrated with forty-three main etched images, forty-two of collieries and drops and a small frontispiece vignette of a whin gin at an unidentified pit (see page 7). The etchings were the work of at least five skilled engravers; Hair himself, J. Brown, S.T. Davies, T.E. Nicholson, and T.A. Prior, working over about five years. A high standard of craftsmanship was maintained throughout the series. All the etchings were taken from Hair's watercolour sketches. The Hatton Gallery possesses forty-two watercolour sketches by Hair depicting aspects of the coal trade. Thirty-seven of these images were used in Hair's book, the remaining five, painted during the same general period as the others, 1828-1842, were not transferred into etchings and have not been reproduced in any form elsewhere (see page 48).

In 1932 the series of watercolours were the property of Mr William Cochrane-Carr, a well known local coal owner and one time president of the North of England Institute of Mining and Mechanical Engineering. Shortly after this time Mr Cochrane-

A keel laden with coal passes beneath the Tyne Bridge around 1840.

Carr presented the watercolours to the Department of Mining Engineering at Armstrong College, now part of the University of Newcastle. For about sixty years the sketches were displayed in the Department of Mining until its closure in the early 1990s, when they were transferred to the Hatton Gallery. There they underwent a thorough programme of restoration and conservation.

The Northumberland and Durham Coalfield

The Great Northern Coalfield was, during the early nineteenth century, the most productive and, in terms of engineering, the most innovative in the world. In 1843, the year before the publication of *Views of the Collieries*, the 192 main collieries of the coalfield employed around 25,770 men and boys, above and below ground. They produced 4,823,967 tons of coal. Many more people were employed as a direct result of the coal trade. These included keelmen and casters, the crews of the colliers, lightermen on the Thames and the factors and agents at the coal exchange.

There were still many years of expansion in the mining industry in the North-East of England ahead. This was facilitated by advancements in mining and railway technology, and driven by the requirement for ever greater quantities of coal to power the growing industries, and as a raw material for many industrial processes. The ready market for good quality coal was not found just in Britain, but in many other European countries. Government figures show the amount of coal shipped out of the Tyne, Wear and Tees in 1848 was around 7,835,490 tons, double the total for five years earlier.

The following pages take a selection of Thomas Hair's watercolours to illustrate the journey of coal from the coalface, through the workings of the mine and the pithead to the wagonways that transported it to the keels and the collier ships on the North-East rivers.

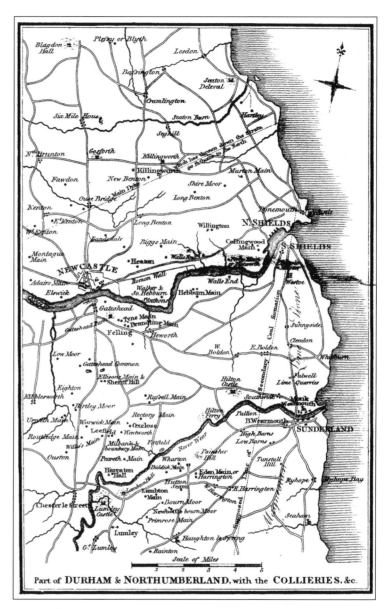

*Part of Durham and Northumberland with the collieries, from **A Treatise on the Coal Mines of Durham and Northumberland**, by J.H.H. Holmes, 1816.*

Crane for Loading the Rollies

Although great technological advances had been made in coal mining during the nineteenth century, the emphasis was still very much on human toil.

'Loading the Rollies' is the first mining process illustrated by Hair. Many labour intensive operations have already taken place before the coal reaches this stage. The coal is dug out of the pit face by hewers, and put into corves by barrow men and coal putters. Each corve, weighing about 560 pounds when full, is drawn and pushed on trams or sledges by dragsmen or foals (the term for a younger boy doing this job and pushing the sledge from behind) towards the pit shaft.

In this sketch, the corves of coal have been brought to a crane underground where they are being loaded onto rollies, low-slung, wheeled trolleys that could carry one or more corves and ran on rails or 'rolleyways'.

Some rolleyways operated by means of an inclined plane mechanism running to the shaft. Increasingly from the mid-1840s the rollies were drawn by steam power. However, in this picture, from the lack of any evidence of an inclined plane or haulage mechanism, it may be safe to assume that the pony provided the power to convey the rollies to and from the shaft.

The artist could have provided a more technical description of what took place at the crane, concentrating on the mechanics of the lifting apparatus. Instead the crane, the rollies and the lifting process are just about visible through the dust and murk. Hair has chosen to explore the effects of light and shadow cast up from a naked flame, possibly a candle, held between the two figures in the centre foreground. The neck and head of the pony are illuminated and stand out in the gloom, as does the handler, who cuts a plucky if not quite heroic stance. Both their shadows are cast up against the wall. Beyond the figures however, 'the sense of utter darkness … is ever present'.

Miners at the coalface from an engraving by Thomas Bewick (1752-1828). Note the candle, the pit props supporting the low roof, and the wooden bucket of coal being carried off.

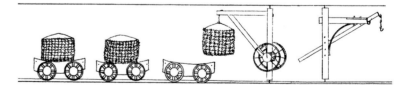

*This drawing from Matthias Dunn's **Winning and Working of Collieries**, 1848, shows how the corves were lifted on to the rollies.*

Bottom of the Shaft, Walbottle Colliery

The rollies have delivered the corves of coal to the bottom of the pit shaft of the Coronation Pit, Walbottle, Northumberland, ready to be lifted up to the surface, 'at bank'.

Although there are several figures in the image and a corve can be seen beginning its journey up the shaft on the end of a chain, once again the artist's main interest is the play of light. A bright glow emanates from the pit shaft into the man-made cavern. This is not daylight streaming in from the surface but light from a burning flare visible at the foot of the shaft. Another source of illumination is the taper held by the seated character. He is about to light a clay pipe, the shape of which is just discernible in his left hand. In spite of the almost casual exposure of naked flame the colliery had been 'remarkably

fortunate in its exemption from explosions'.

By the early 1840s wicker corves were being 'fast superseded by the adoption of square tubs, made of wood or iron with wheels attached'. Tubs ran on the rolleyways and made the rollies redundant. Rather than being hauled by a rope or chain to the surface, tubs were, 'conducted up the shaft upon cages or cradles, sliding between guides of wood extending from the top to the bottom of even the deepest pits'. This made for greater efficiency, reducing much of the time and effort spent handling the coal underground and on the surface.

It is clear from the accompanying text in Hair's book that there was an awareness of the very latest engineering developments in the mining industry, but here, as in a number of other illustrations in the series, perhaps because the sketches were made over a number of years during which innovations were taking place, older technology is represented rather than the new. Old fashioned methods or not, in 1837 the Coronation Pit dispatched a very healthy 52,162 tons of its 'Holywell Main' coal to London via the staith at Lemington on the Tyne.

In 1859 Walter White, described his impressions of the bottom of the shaft at East Holywell pit.

*This illustration from W. Fordyce's **History of Coal, Coke, Coalfields** 1860, was 'modernised' from Thomas Hair's etching, and clumsily substitutes wheeled tubs and a cage for the rollies and corves. Fordyce was keen to show current working practice.*

…we were seated at one side of a great tunnel-like excavation stretching to unknown distances to the right and left, opening immediately in front of us upon the foot of the shaft, and containing a tramway, along which the wagons were drawn, and pushed to the cage. Above my head, fixed to the black wall of shale or stone, whichever it might be, hung two flaring oil lamps … I could see a constant stream of smoke creeping to the shaft, and there passing up as though a chimney …

(Walter White, *Northumberland and the Border*, 1859.)

The C Pit, Hebburn Colliery

This is an extremely useful general view of a colliery that describes many of the structures and activities that could be found at the pithead or bank. Standing tall in the centre of the scene is the head gear located directly over the pit shaft. To the left of this are the buildings housing the winding engines that powered the lifting operation in the shaft. Ropes from the winding engine can be seen travelling over the winding wheel and down through the head gear. To the right of the engine house is the large form of the ventilation funnel marked by the presence of a large vane. Further to the right, beyond the head gear are the screens where coal was graded.

Not all collieries shared the same configuration of buildings and equipment on the surface. Size and design varied from pit to pit to accommodate the needs of that particular working. One form of winding gear was the horse powered whin gin, a low-tech but effective solution to hauling corves, men and equipment up and down the pit shaft. It was well suited to smaller or poorer collieries.

Empty corves are seen being readied for their return into the pit. At bank the full corves would be unhooked from the rope or chain by the banksman and transferred across to the screens where they would be emptied, and the coal sent on the next phase of its journey.

The sinking of Hebburn Colliery began in 1792. The pit acquired a notorious reputation for underground explosions. It was following a visit to Hebburn and experiments with gases from the pit, that Humphrey Davy developed his safety lamp for miners, the Davy Lamp, in 1815. Prior to this, lighting in mines had been provided by the naked flame of candles – not to be recommended in explosive environments. From about 1750 the steel mill was used in many pits. This was a device that created a stream of shimmering sparks as a flint was drawn across a revolving steel wheel. Again this was far from ideal in mines that suffered from fire damp. The luminosity of the sparks would change as gas built up, so the miners perhaps had some warning of potential dangers. Although the Davy Lamp provided a safer means of lighting the underground workings it was itself not without problems and could explode under certain conditions. A better solution to the menace of explosions in the mines would be, as one commentator noted, 'sought in more efficient means of ventilation'.

There had been a number of relatively effective attempts to pump air from mines using what might be generically termed 'pipes'. The most common form of ventilation in Hair's time was provided by furnaces or burning fire baskets, often set at the foot of pit shafts to created an updraft. Foul air would be drawn up and out of the workings, sometimes through separate ventilation or 'upcast shafts'. Often, however, it was drawn through the main and only shaft, divided from the clean air in the 'downcast shaft' by bratticing (a wooden partition). Underground, trappers – children often as young as five – regulated the flow of air in the mine by opening and closing trap doors between sections of the pit.

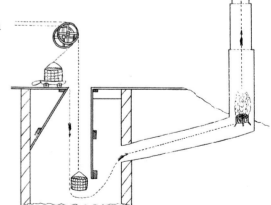

Matthias Dunn's drawing of a ventilation shaft, 1848.

Hebburn Colliery the G. Pit.

Thos H Hair 1838

The Pumping Engine at Friar's Goose

Explosive gasses were not the only hazard facing the coal mines in the North-East. Often there was a problem with mine water hampering operations. If this was left unchecked it could even flood the workings completely. Pumping engines of various designs were engaged to draw water from the pits. The engine at Friar's Goose, just east of Gateshead, was, in the mid 1800s, the most powerful on the Tyne. Its three sets of pumps were capable of lifting almost one and a half million gallons of water per day and bringing it more than three hundred feet from the bottom of the mine to the surface. The dimensions and performance of the machinery remains impressive:

[Each] cylinder is 6 feet in diameter, in which the stroke is 9 feet… At each stroke, about 195 gallons of water are delivered at bank; and, as the average is 6 strokes per minute, 1170 gallons are delivered in that space of time …

Hair's book includes a contemporary description of the interior of a working engine house:

You now see from the upper part of the engine house a huge beam, protruding itself like a giant's arm, alternatively lifting itself up, and then falling again. To this beam is attached the rod and bucket of a pump, which probably at some hundred yards deep, is lifting out the water from the mine.

All the sights and sounds of the working coalfield made a great impression on visitors, and some, like the writer William Howitt in his chronicle of his journey through the North-East, reported their experiences with much enthusiasm:

Wherever reared themselves those tall engine houses there also towered aloft two vapoury columns, one of black smoke, and one near it of white steam. These neighbouring columns, like the ghosts of Ossian, slanted themselves in the wind and waved spectre-like in the air, each like some demon with a pale spirit in his keeping, whom he is compelling to enormous labours; and such noises filled them as seemed to confirm the belief of it. Some of these engines were groaning, some puffing, some making the most unearthly sighings and yawnings, as if the very Gouls and Afrits of the Eastern stories were set to stupendous labours and were doing them in despair.

Of all the structures found at the collieries and staiths which Hair captured in his series of watercolour sketches, only the pumping engine house at Friar's Goose survives. Thankfully the building was subject to an extensive renovation a few years ago and can be visited today.

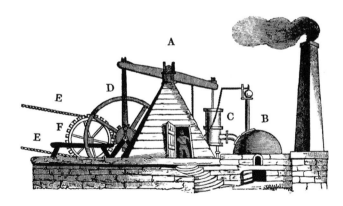

*John Holland, in his book **Fossil Fuel, the Collieries and Coal Trade of Great Britain**, 1841, describes one of the 'old-fashioned steam-engines still very common … and called a whim, or whimsey.' This type of engine might be used for raising corves or pumping water.*

Friars Goose Pumping Engine

Thos. H. Hair

The Phoenix Pit, Old Etherley

The Phoenix Pit was situated about three miles west of Bishop Auckland in the south of County Durham. This area had been 'a long neglected district of the Durham Coalfield' although coal had been a well established element of the local economy for at least six hundred years. Records confirm that mining had been practised on Cockfield Fell since the early 1300s. That this quarter of the coalfield was under-exploited was in the main due to lack of adequate means of transporting the coal to the growing industrial and domestic markets. Before the building of the Stockton and Darlington railway and its numerous branch lines from 1825, coal from this area was carried by cart, pony or pack mule. The Stockton and Darlington railway connected south-west Durham to the staiths at Port Clarence and at Middlesbrough on the river Tees.

Illustrated here are the screens at the Phoenix where coal was graded for size and separated from any foreign material such as shale. The wheel at the top of the head gear is visible over the roof of the screens. Close proximity of the screens to the shaft was important to reduce time and effort in processing the coal. Not all of the coal brought up from the pit was of the required size or quality for the market. In earlier times, and still at poorer pits in the 1840s, the sorting and grading of coal was done entirely by hand and often by women. The use of screens improved the process and introduced a greater degree of consistency to the grading of coal for size. Stone still had to be removed by hand.

Early screens were constructed from wood but were later replaced with metal. They were a simple arrangement of bars or grates running in parallel set, 'about half an inch asunder', which allowed small coal and dust to fall through. It is possible to determine in Hair's sketch that the apparatus was tilted at about forty-five degrees to regulate to fall of the coal towards the bottom of the screen from where it was placed into the wagons waiting below. It must be remembered that the colliery owners had no interest in incurring the costs of bringing small coal and stone, which was to them of no value, out of the pits. To help prevent this, by 1800, the owners had introduced a system of fines that would be levied against the pitmen according to the amount of small coal and other waste carried to the surface. This was another effective, if rather crude, system of quality control. In later years, with the growth in the need for coke for industrial processes, small coal developed a commercial worth.

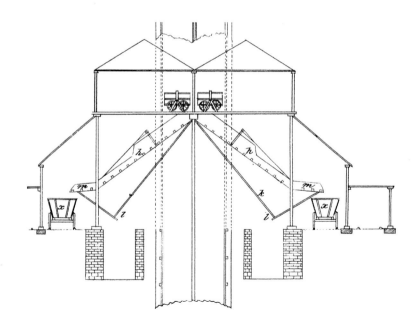

*Screens, illustrated here from Matthias Dunn's **Winning and Working of Collieries**, 1848, were usually sixteen to twenty-feet in height.*

On April 23, 1810 the first coal from St Hilda's was 'conveyed to the spout, amidst great rejoicing'. Just over nineteen years later, on 28 June 1839, the mood at the colliery was of despair. An explosion in the workings, blamed on fire damp coming into contact with the naked flame of a candle, left fifty-one miners dead. Many of the workers died from the effects of choke damp, sometimes called 'carbonic acid gas', that often succeeded explosions in mines. Thomas Hair describes the scene as reported:

The mute despair, or frantic grief of the assembled parents, wives, children and friends were intensely agonising; and as the bodies of the sufferers were one by one brought to bank, and conveyed in carts to their recent homes, the scene became almost too painful for contemplation.

There were many acts of courage from rescuers who entered and re-entered the pit regardless for the safety of their own lives. A local wine merchant called Mather went into the mine shortly after the catastrophe occurred and worked helping the injured until they could be retrieved. A witness described the devastation he saw when he descended into the workings:

The deadly gas became stronger as we approached. We encountered in one place five dead bodies who had died from the effects of the gas – without one muscle of the face distorted. Then there were three more, that had been destroyed by the explosion … cloths burnt and torn – the hair singed – the skin and flesh torn away in several places, with an expression as if the spirit passed away in agony … We encountered two men, one with a light, the other bearing something on his shoulders; it was a blackened mass – a poor, dead, burnt boy he was taking out. A little further on we found wagons that had been loaded, overturned bottom upwards, scattered in different directions; a horse lying dead,

directly in a passage, with his head turned over his shoulder, as if, in falling, he made his last effort to escape.

One man assisting in the rescue was overcome by the choke damp and brought out of the mine:

He was questioned as to how he felt. "I am not very well sir," said he. "I have two sons in there", pointing down to the place he had been driven from in his attempts to recover his children. "One was 16, the other 22."

The youngest to die in the tragedy were Thomas Elstob aged nine, and the sons of G. Longstaff, aged nine and eleven. The oldest was Thomas Horn aged fifty-seven.

A public meeting was held at South Shields Town Hall to set up a fund for the benefit of the families of the victims. There were nineteen widows and forty-four children left without support and the *Newcastle Daily Courant* of 5 July 1839 reported that £400 was quickly collected. A committee was also formed to make enquiries into the best means for ventilating mines.

The watercolour was titled by the artist 'St. Hilda's, Wallsend'. 'Wallsend' referred to the high quality coal – of Wallsend standard – produced at the pit.

AWFUL LOSS OF LIFE AT SOUTH SHIELDS
EXPLOSION AT ST.HILDA'S COLLIERY

The headline in the Newcastle Daily Courant, 5 July 1839, a week after the explosion.

St Hilda's Wallsend

Thos. H. Hair 1839

27

It was the coal from the collieries of Wallsend upon Tyne that set the benchmark for quality on the national and international markets in the early nineteenth century. The attributes of Wallsend coal were described as follows:

... [it] kindles easily ... in burning, it cakes or runs together, but not to such a hard solid mass as some other sorts, emitting at the same time, a great deal of heat as well as smoke and flame; it leaves a small quantity of residuum or ashes.

Any coal that achieved the standard 'Wallsend' was readily bought on the exchange: 'The designation 'Wallsend Coal' has continued for many years [to be] a passport to the quickest sale and the highest prices' says Hair.

As a result, other mining areas in England and Scotland often used the label 'Wallsend' to their own advantage at the exchange. To distinguish the real thing from the imitation, coal from Wallsend collieries adopted other designations. For example, coal from the Church Pit was called for some time 'Russell's Wallsend' after the mine owner at that time, William Russell, or 'Bensham Wallsend' or 'Bensham Main', after the particular seam yielding the best coal.

The text accompanying Hair's image of the Church Pit gives a broad description of the scene and a flavour of the language used at the time;

The view of Church Pit ... comprises nearly all the paraphernalia of an extensive colliery ... On the railway front, the efficiency of that mode of transmission is exemplified by the fact of a ponderous wagon full of coals being moved on a gentle incline by the hand of a single individual. A railway from another colliery [Killingworth] crosses the above by means of a wooden bridge ... Behind and in the centre, is the 'shaft frame' [head gear] supporting pulleys that overhang the pit. Over these wheels the
ropes are passed by which men, corves and coal are lowered or raised, to or from the bottom of the mine. Contiguous is a lofty brick chimney or funnel, attached to the upcast shaft, and having a smoke dispenser at the top, through which the impure air from the workings is ejected ... On the right is the engine house for working the ropes; and close adjoining are the boilers, & c.; wherein is generated that immense power which raises all the produce of the pit to the surface.

Wagons from the Church Pit made their journey to the staith on the Tyne down a self acting incline. Full wagons were attached to a rope in a loop guided by pulleys. At the other end of the rope, down towards the river, empty wagons that had delivered their coal to the staiths were hooked on. The weight of the full wagons travelling down the incline drew the empty wagons back up to the pit. This was a very efficient use of energy.

PRICES OF COALS:

Delivered to any part of Newcastle, warranted free from dirt, and weight guaranteed.

PER LOAD OF 15 CWT.

	Near Depot.	Centre.	Any Part.
Lady Windsor's best selected	5 6	5 9	6 0
Original Tanfield's Wallsend	5 6	5 9	6 0
Marley Hill Main Coal	4 6	4 9	5 0
Clavering's Main Do.	4 6	4 9	5 0
Thirds of superior quality	3 9	4 0	4 3

Coal prices of Joseph Liddell, coke, coal, and iron merchant of Scotswood Road, from Ward's Directory for 1850. His coal came from Tanfield in County Durham, but was still 'Wallsend' quality.

Tho H Hair 1838

The Church Pit Wallsend

The Jubilee Pit, Coxlodge

Named to commemorate the fiftieth jubilee of the reign of George III, the Jubilee Pit, Coxlodge, was about four and a half miles north of Newcastle.

A number of wagons or chaldrons of coal are waiting to be sent on their way from the colliery to the staiths on the Tyne. A 'Newcastle chaldron' would hold around two and a half tons of coal. From Coxlodge, horses hauled the wagons for about a mile until they met the wagonway from Gosforth Colliery. For the remaining three and a half miles to the river they were 'drawn thither principally by fixed engines'. Fixed engines were steam haulage engines set, usually at the top of inclines, adjacent to rail or wagonways. Wagons were connected to the hauling apparatus by long ropes or chains and pulled up the banks. They might be sent down the other side under their own weight or on a self acting incline plane arrangement.

There is no report of steam locomotion being used at Coxlodge at this time, although many years earlier there had been experiments at the pit with a steam engine designed by John Blenkinsop. Although the test of September 1813 failed to achieve the anticipated speed of three and a half miles per hour drawing sixteen full chaldrons with a combined weight of seventy tons, Hair's book describes it as successful. Successful or otherwise:

After the experiment was finished, a large party of gentlemen connected with coal mining partook of an excellent dinner provided at the grand stand for the occasion, when the afternoon was spent in the most agreeable and convivial manner.

Underground, no doubt, the toil went on.

Beyond the pit there is a glimpse of a row of pit cottages almost situated 'at bank'. If there was colliery housing available to the miners and their families, it went with the job. The miners had no rights of tenancy if they ceased working for the pit. In reality miners had few rights at all, and tied housing gave the mine owners even greater power over their workers. However neat the row of cottages may appear, housing conditions for mining folk in the early nineteenth century rarely rose above being squalid, 'confined and dismal'. Too often there was no proper sanitation or even rudimentary drainage and families were without a convenient fresh water supply.

Between rows of houses might be found 'one long ash heap and dung hill'. The dwellings were usually poorly constructed, extremely damp, smoky and overcrowded. Many families, not sufficiently privileged to enjoy even these poor conditions, had to endure life in temporary shanties.

During the late 1820s a young doctor called Thomas Wright was assistant to a surgeon in the Newcastle area and often attended patients in the nearby mining villages. He describes pit housing in the village of Heaton:

The pitmen's houses are generally built in long rows of two houses in breadth each containing one room a garret and a pantry. The overmen and those who have large families or who are favourites may obtain two rooms, perhaps three, as some of the houses are so built for the purpose. These are furnished according to the disposition or means of the occupier but one thing is uniformly good – the fire … In many instances large masses of high built houses are rented by the colliery and separate rooms portioned out to each family. Every householder is provided with a small garden and generally keeps a pig or two, fat bacon being a favourite dish.

(From *Diary of a Doctor: Surgeon's Assistant in Newcastle* edited by Alistair Johnson, Newcastle Libraries, 1998)

The Jubilee Pit Carlodge

J H Hair 1838

Broomside Colliery

This broad landscape view of Broomside Colliery, about three miles from Hetton in County Durham, is typical of a number of Hair's representations of collieries. The artist presents a more distant aspect of the colliery, in a pastoral setting. Sheep graze on the valley sides, stooks of corn stand in a distant field, trees and hedgerows map out the tranquil landscape. Amongst all this, the structures of the pit and the adjacent railway line, represent the progress of the industrial age.

Often today we associate coal mines with industrial sprawl, but this was rarely the case even into the twentieth century. The vast majority of collieries were located in the green and pleasant rolling countryside and the communities that grew around them seldom developed beyond the status of village. A visit to No Place or Quaking Houses in County Durham, or many of the numerous other former colliery sites in the North-East confirm this.

Describing how visitors to the coalfield might be taken aback when confronted with first sight of the coal industry, and in particular by the various forms of railway, one traveller noted:

Amid all these uncouth sounds and sights, the voice of a cuckoo or corncrake came at intervals to assure me that I was still on earth, and not conjured into some land of insane wheels and machinery possessed by riotous spirits.

Coal from Broomside was taken to drops at Seaham Harbour along the Durham and Sunderland Railway. Particularly interesting in this scene are the wagons being hauled up the incline by a standing engine. Bringing up the rear of the wagons on the right are two covered passenger carriages. This is one of two images by Hair depicting passengers being carried in this way. The other is the 'Engine at Pittington', illustrated here, where a train can be seen in the background.

The idea of passenger rail transport was well established by the time Hair's book was published. The steam passenger railway line between Liverpool and Manchester had opened in 1830. Here, however, we have passengers on a colliery line. William Fordyce explained: 'Covered vans were attached to the coal trains and passengers conveyed from Sunderland to Durham by the railway belonging to the colliery'.

The Pittington Engine.

Broomside Colliery.
Tho.ᵗ H Hair 1839

The Old Locomotive Engine, Wylam

Steam locomotives were developed initially to serve the needs of industry, but operators were swift to spot the commercial potential of transporting passengers. The locomotive in Hair's sketch was built in 1813 by William Hedley. At that time Hedley was employed by Christopher Blackett as the viewer at the Wylam Colliery in the Tyne valley, on what was at that time the western edge of the Northumberland coalfield.

Hedley's first locomotive preceded that of George Stephenson, who was born in Wylam, by about a year. A Cornishman, Richard Trevethick, is credited with the first application of a steam locomotive in Wales in 1804. This utilised a cogged wheel and 'third' rail to haul itself along. Hedley successfully proved that the friction between the locomotive's wheels and the iron rails would be sufficient to allow the engine to pull substantial loads without the need for a cog system. At least two locomotives of a similar design were developed by Hedley at Wylam.

Puffing Billy, an early Wylam locomotive, built in 1813, can be seen in the Science Museum in London and *Wylam Dilley*, another original engine, in the Royal Museum of Scotland, Edinburgh. The Hedley family was later connected with the colliery at Craghead, County Durham, and *Dilley* was transferred from Wylam to Craghead in the 1860s. One author claims the engine in Hair's picture is *Puffing Billy*, but this may well be inaccurate.

In 1836 Hedley explained that his original locomotive: 'drew eight loaded coal wagons after it at a rate of four to five miles an hour on the Wylam railroad which was in a very bad state'. Each wagon weighed over two tons when full and they made the five mile journey from the colliery to the staiths at Lemington on rails with a six foot gauge. At Lemington the coal was loaded into keels and carried down the Tyne to be loaded onto waiting colliers. The height of the old stone bridge at Newcastle prevented the larger colliers from venturing further up stream.

Hair chose to depict a locomotive that, although still functioning effectively, was by the 1840s rather out of date. The artist seems to relish the configuration of the piston rods, beams and cylinders and the smoke and steam puffing from the stack. Once again Hair demonstrates pleasure in the play of light. Flames lick from the open fire box at the front of the locomotive and cast onto the attendant engineer and the ground beneath. By the line, a group of men gather around a burning fire lamp. The wagons catch the light of the lamp as they trundle to the staith.

*Wylam Dilley, temporarily converted into a steam tug and escorted by soldiers, takes keels down the Tyne during the keelmen's strike of 1822. (**Monthly Chronicle, August 1887.**)*

Old Locomotive Engine
Wylam Coll⁫y.

Thos H. Hair.

Hetton Colliery

The early history of steam locomotion is dominated by the name of George Stephenson even though a number of other engineers 'got there first'. Profiting from the work of pioneers such as Hedley, Stephenson produced his first locomotive at Killingworth Colliery, Northumberland, in 1814 and went on to become an engineering legend. The working life of Stephenson's locomotives surpasses even that of Hedley's *Wylam Dilley*. One of the Hetton engines, though much modified, was still in service at the colliery in 1908.

> *Five of Mr. Stephenson's patent travelling engines … went into service at the Hetton Colliery, approximately six miles north east of Durham City in 1822, after the opening of the wagon way from [the] colliery to the staiths on the Wear.*

The line at Hetton was worked partly by locomotives and partly by fixed engines to haul wagons up the more difficult inclines. The smoking stack of a working engine can be seen poking out over the pit heap in the centre of the image. Another locomotive stands deserted in front of the heap. In 1825, a few years before this sketch was made, 'it was rumoured that the locomotives at Hetton were to be abandoned …' in preference for fixed engines. Hair may be making a visual reference to this by including an idle locomotive.

Hetton Colliery was extremely significant in that it was the first to work coal under the magnesian limestone of County Durham, thus leading to the development of mining throughout East Durham from the 1820s to the 1980s. Hair states that: 'Before its commencement, there was not a house within a mile of the spot, which now teems with a numerous population'. The sinking of a pit would create a local boom bringing in miners and their families and all the services they might need. Once the coal at a particular pit was exhausted, the coal mining community gathered about it might need to move on if no other work could be found nearby: 'Houses and pits were often simultaneously abandoned, and the place presents a desolate appearance'.

The miners of County Durham are described by William Morrison of Chester-le-Street in his evidence for the Children's Employment Commission, 1842.

> *The 'outward man' distinguishes a pitman from every other operative. His stature is diminutive, his figure disproportionate and misshapen; his legs much bowed; his chest protruding … his forehead low and retreating; his habit is tainted with scrofula … I never saw a jolly looking pitman.*

The above is in contrast to John Holland's 1841 description of Northumberland miners, who reputedly had a taste for flamboyant dress when out of the pit.

> *Their holiday waistcoats, called by them posey jackets, were frequently of very curious patterns, displaying flowers of various dyes: their stockings mostly blue, purple, pink, or mixed colours. A great part of them used to have their hair very long … when drest in their best attire it was commonly spread over their shoulders. Some of them of them wore two or three narrow ribbons round their hats … in which it was customary for them to insert … primroses or other flowers. Perhaps it will strike a stranger, on passing along the streets of Newcastle on a Sunday or holiday, that the better sort of the inhabitants are partial to poseys or flowers.*

Hetton Colliery
Th.^s H. Hair

Pemberton Main

Work on the siting of Pemberton Main Colliery (later known as Wearmouth Colliery, and now the Stadium of Light) on the north bank of the river Wear at Sunderland began in 1826. When opened it was the deepest pit in the world at around 1,500 feet to the Bensham seam. Pemberton Main dispensed with the use of corves to draw coal from the workings and employed a seven foot high metal tub that could hold up to a ton and a half at a time (a corve held around one fifth of a ton). Miners and their equipment were also conveyed in the tub, suspended by a rope that was itself five tons in weight.

The great depth of the pit meant that the average temperature in the workings was between seventy and eighty degrees fahrenheit. The heat was believed to cause a particularly unpleasant 'species of boil' which affected many of Pemberton Main's pitmen in their first few months of working underground.

Hair is not interested simply in the arrangement of the structures at the pithead; the colliery represents only an element in a broader panorama of life along the river.

The colliery had been working for about fifteen years before this sketch was made in 1841. A well established spoil heap has grown across the bank side. Four wagons travel on the incline leading to the drops just half a mile away. Below the colliery, on the river bank, ship building is underway, possibly the building of colliers. Five keel boats make their way down stream on the receding tide. A keel could carry up to '8 Newcastle chaldrons [wagons] or 21 tons'. They were used to transport coal from the reaches of the river which were too shallow for navigation by colliers.

On the Tyne a keel would usually be crewed by three men ('keel bullies') and a boy (a 'pee dee') and on the Wear by one man and a boy. This was due to the different working practices on the two rivers. Keelmen on the Tyne transferred the coal into the colliers themselves. On the Wear the transfer was carried out by a separate class of labourer called a 'caster', no doubt derived from the action of casting coal from the keels. The keels passing Pemberton Main appear short-crewed even by the standards of the Wear. The design of keels on the two rivers also varied. Those on the Wear had a shallower draught, but were longer and squarer than the boats on the Tyne. In this illustration the keels resemble small barges. When not utilising the flow and tide of the river, keels were propelled in a variety of ways, by sail, or rowing using long oars or by a form of punting with a long pole or 'puoy'.

Although the keelmen were, more than once, provoked into violent disorder when their trade was threatened, particularly by the introduction of the loading of mechanised drops on the rivers to load colliers, a contemporary writer praised them as being: 'hardy and laborious ... distinguished for their great muscular strength ... loud and vociferous ... yet their conduct is uniformly civil and exemplary'.

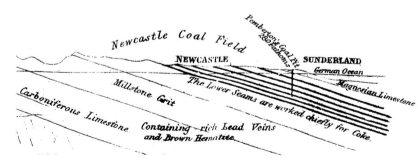

*A section of the Northern Coalfield from William Fordyce's **History of Coal, Coke, Coalfields**, 1860. The Pemberton Pit at 280 fathoms depth is noted.*

Pemberton Main Colly.
Thos H Hair 1839

The Drops at Wallsend

New technology in loading colliers saw large reductions in the numbers of keelmen required. Towards the end of the eighteenth century the coal trade on the Tyne employed about 1,600 keelmen. By 1827 this number was reduced to 850, almost all of them engaged in bringing coal down river from pits above the Tyne Bridge.

Drops were the mechanism by which coal was transferred directly from the wagons which brought it to the river into collier ships. Coal was shipped to London, the Continent, Scandinavia and beyond. The international nature of the coal trade is emphasised in Hair's book – the explanation of this image describes 'a Scottish ship at the staith and a French vessel waiting her turn'.

Hair also provides a good description of a working drop:

Lofty timber framing projecting deep into the water. At its extremity is fixed a drop, consisting of a square frame hung together upon pulleys, and counterbalanced by back weights [one of which is visible suspended just above the river]. The loaded wagon, together with the square frame, descends by its own gravity to the hatchway of the vessel, delivers its coal and in turn the empty wagon is returned by means of the balance weights, the motion in both cases being regulated by a brake wheel. A man is lowered down with the wagon, whose business it is to unhasp its moveable bottom and thereby let the coal drop into the hold of the vessel.

Another contemporary writer commented upon the 'picturesque appearance' of the wagons in descent.

The system was designed by William Chapman of Newcastle upon Tyne, 'who took out a patent for it about the year 1800'. According to Hair, Chapman received little, if any, remuneration or acknowledgement from those who later adopted or adapted his invention, yet the savings in manpower and loading time of colliers were enormous.

Below the drop, protruding out towards the river at about forty-five degrees, is an elongated wooden spout down which coal could be fed into smaller vessels and keels, via a hole between the railway lines. Traps and hanging doors were placed in the inside of the spout reducing the speed of the coal's descent and reducing breakages to the precious commodity.

A description of a working drop, from **Fossil Fuel, the Collieries and Coal Trade of Great Britain**, *by John Holland, 1841.*

A: Platform where the railroad ends. B: Shed containing four pulleys. C: Flat ropes attached to D, a lever. E: bolts. F: Flat ropes. G: Long timber levers. H: Weight consisting of cast iron slabs. I: Waggon. K: Staithsman controlling descent of waggon by a brake. L: Spout. M: Tackle to regulate matter passing down the spout.

Drops at Wallsend

Benwell Staith

Here Hair captures a quality of atmosphere not matched by any other image in the series. There is a feeling of calm, if not quite tranquillity, about the light mist hanging over the river at low tide and it is possible to imagine the gentle slop of the keel boats' oars as they enter the water.

Benwell staith was situated on the River Tyne little more that two miles up stream from Newcastle and only a short distance from Benwell colliery. It was here, according to Hair, that, 'the first drop used for lowering wagons down to the keels and ships was erected in 1808'. This is disputed by some historians and commentators who place the first drop at Wallsend in 1810.

The illustration shows a coal spout which funnelled coal into boats. The squared form of the spout is visible protruding beyond the stone building. There are two vessels tied up at the staith. One is positioned directly under the spout, ready to receive coal. Naturally, neither boat approaches the tonnage of the colliers at Wallsend.

The coals are conveyed by inclined planes from the pits to the staith, where they are put into keels to be carried to the ships lying below Newcastle bridge and at Shields.

The low bridge at Newcastle at this time restricted the size of vessel that could venture further up stream.

On the staith a wagon is approaching the spout. Standing on the back of the wagon is a brakesman controlling its speed by the application of a simple brake lever device.

Fearing that their trade would suffer because of mechanised loading of ships, keelmen on the Tyne attempted, on several occasions, to close the staiths by legal action. They claimed that the structures were a hazard to navigation for river users. Not surprisingly, the litigation failed.

To the rear of the staith, attached to the side one of the buildings, is a working water wheel. We are not told by Hair what function the buildings had, or what purpose the wheel served. There was a lead works adjacent to the Benwell colliery that poured lead down one of the old pit shafts. Perhaps the wheel was related to this.

*Wagon and brakesman. (From **Fossil Fuel, the Collieries and Coal Trade of Great Britain**, by John Holland, 1841.)*

Benwell Staith.

43

Staiths with spouts were first constructed at this location, Galleys Gill, also known as Lambton's Drops, in 1812. They served the expanding wagonway system that linked the inland mines to the ports. To reach the far end of the staith, wagons were taken through a tunnel cut into the cliff face. The tunnel is visible to the right of the picture. In the distance it is just possible to make out the conical chimney of the glass works, standing in front of the elegant iron bridge.

The design of the drops on the Wear differed from those at Wallsend on the Tyne and this can easily be seen by comparing this plate with page 41. Hair explains that at Sunderland:

the wagon [is] suspended from the extremity of a strong framing of beams, which turns on a central axle, and lowers its load to the deck of the vessel.

The Reverend T.F. Dibdin in his *Tour in the Northern Counties of England*, 1838, described the effect of the dust from the staiths on the landscape and people of the locality:

Houses, windows, walls, pillars, posts and posterns, were all more or less veiled in what may be delicately designated black crape. Even the human countenance seemed to partake of it…

Hair declared, that around the area of the drops, there were: 'Twenty dirty faces to a clean one!'

Increasing use of drops and spouts to load the colliers created a great deal of consternation amongst the keelmen and casters on the Wear as it did on the Tyne, as they saw their jobs under threat. Hair records that the eleven drops at Galleys Gill were: 'capable of shipping 150 keels per day'. The two trades were forced into industrial action on numerous occasions in what were increasingly vain efforts to preserve their livelihoods. On March 20th 1815, following the announcement that there were imminent plans to extend the staiths at Sunderland, uproar and violence ensued:

A great number of persons [predominantly keelmen and casters] assembled in a riotous manner and proceeded to pull down the wooden bridge … They also set fire to the depot and machinery for lowering the wagons down the inclined plane; and one house in the neighbourhood was pulled down and several others unroofed. Many persons were injured … and one man was killed.

Order was only restored when late into the night, 'a party of Dragoons arrived from Newcastle, and dispersed the mob'.

Drops at Sunderland
Thos H Hair.

The opening of the Stockton and Darlington Railway in 1825 and the development of its numerous branch lines, enabled the inland coalfield of south Durham to be more fully exploited. Large quantities of coal could be transported with relative ease to the staiths for the coastal and export trades.

Middlesbrough, on the south side of the river Tees, owed its origins to the railway. It was recognised that the greater depth of water at this point of the river would accommodate larger vessels than could be facilitated up stream at Stockton. The railway terminated here, and the drops were opened in 1831, although by the time Hair's book was published in 1844, the drops had been 'superseded by docks'.

The design of the drops on the Tees was rather different from those on either the Tyne or Wear. The picture shows that the drops were huge enclosed structures that towered above the waiting colliers. Another peculiarity of the design was that the wagons had to be: 'raised by a steam engine from the railway to the upper floor of the staith, and thence lowered again to the decks of the vessels in the river.'

Hair has provided a distant view of the drops across the quiet waters of the Tees. Amongst the activity along the staiths, are two steam paddle tugs. They helped to manoeuvre the colliers into position beneath the drops

and then out again towards the open sea.

In the foreground is the ferry crossing the Tees from Port Clarence, illustrated below. Port Clarence was the termination point of another line, the Clarence railway, built to serve the pits of southern Durham.

Beyond the staith the tall chimney seen towering in the distance marks the 'extensive iron forges and engine building of Messrs. Bolckow and Vaughan'.

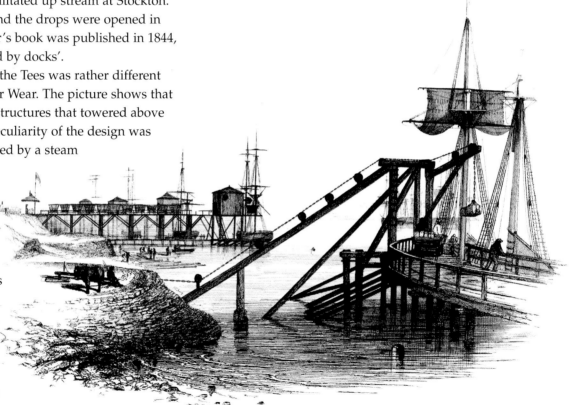

The Clarence Drops on the Tees.

Tho. H. Hair

Drop on the Tees at Middlesbro

Sources, and Further Reading

Frank Atkinson, *The Great Northern Coalfield 1700-1900*, Durham County Local History Society, 1966, 1968.

T.F. Dibdin, *A Bibliographical, Antiquarian and Picturesque Tour in the Northern Counties of England*, 1838.

Matthias Dunn, *Winning and Working of Collieries*, 1848.

W. Fordyce, *A History of Coal, Coke, Coalfields*, 1860.

P.E.H. Hair (Ed.) *Coals on Rails or the Reason of my Wrighting: The Autobiography of Anthony Errington*, Liverpool University Press, 1988.

Thomas H. Hair, *Views of the Collieries in the Counties of Northumberland and Durham*, 1844, reprinted 1969.

Marshall Hall, *The Artists of Northumbria*, Marshall Hall Associates, 1973, 1982

John Holland, *Fossil Fuel, the Collieries and Coal Trade of Great Britain*, 1841.

J.H.H. Holmes, *A Treatise on the Coal Mines ...*, 1816.

William Howitt, *Journeys to Remarkable Places*, 1842.

Alastair Johnson (Ed.) *Diary of a Doctor: Surgeon's Assistant in Newcastle 1826-1829, by Thomas Giordani Wright*, Newcastle Libraries, 1998.

Dick Keys and Ken Smith, *Black Diamonds by Sea: North-East Sailing Colliers, 1780-1880*, Newcastle Libraries, 1998.

J.R. Liefchild, *Our Coal and Our Coal-Pits*, 1853.

Edwin Miller, (Ed.) *Eyewitness: The Industrial Revolution in the North East*, 1968.

Walter White, *Northumberland and the Border*, 1859.

Nicholas Wood, *A Practical Treatise on Rail-Roads*, 1825.

Burdon Main Colliery, near North Shields, 1839, one of the watercolours not reproduced as an etching.